Police Cars
on the Go

by Anne J. Spaight

BUMBA BOOKS™

LERNER PUBLICATIONS ◆ MINNEAPOLIS

Note to Educators:

Throughout this book, you'll find critical thinking questions. These can be used to engage young readers in thinking critically about the topic and in using the text and photos to do so.

Lerner Publications Company
A division of Lerner Publishing Group, Inc.
241 First Avenue North
Minneapolis, MN 55401 USA

For reading levels and more information, look up this title at www.lernerbooks.com.

Library of Congress Cataloging-in-Publication Data

The Cataloging-in-Publication Data for *Police Cars on the Go* is on file at the Library of Congress.
ISBN 978-1-5124-1449-3 (lib. bdg.)
ISBN 978-1-5124-1489-9 (pbk.)
ISBN 978-1-5124-1490-5 (EB pdf)

Manufactured in the United States of America
1 – VP – 7/15/16

LERNER
SOURCE

Expand learning beyond the printed book. Download free, complementary educational resources for this book from our website, www.lerneresource.com.

Table of Contents

Police Cars

Police officers keep us safe.

They use police cars to do

their jobs.

Officers drive around

a city.

They stop unsafe drivers.

Why is it good
to stop unsafe
drivers?

Officers catch criminals.

Police cars take the criminals away.

They go to the police station.

Police cars have loud sirens.

They have flashing lights.

Sirens and lights tell other drivers

that the police are near.

Drivers move out of the way.

Police cars are fast.

Officers can drive quickly.

They come when people

need help.

Why is it helpful for police cars to be fast?

12

Police cars have radios.

Officers talk to each other on the radios.

They call for more help if they need it.

Dogs help some officers do their jobs.

Some police cars have a space for dogs.

How might dogs help police officers do their jobs?

Police cars drive in
parades.

Kids get to look inside
the cars.

20

Police cars are very useful.

The police use them to keep

us safe.

Parts of a Police Car

lights

wheels

Picture Glossary

criminals

people who break the law

flashing

going on and off

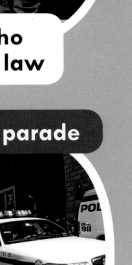

parade

an event where cars drive through the streets to celebrate a special day

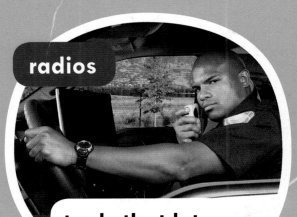

radios

tools that let people talk to each other over long distances

23

Index

Read More

Bellisario, Gina. *Let's Meet a Police Officer.* Minneapolis: Millbrook Press, 2013.

Murray, Julie. *Police Cars.* Minneapolis: Abdo Kids, 2016.

Siemens, Jared. *Police Officers.* New York: AV2 by Weigl, 2015.

Photo Credits